Fuck Off

ICE CREAM SWEAR

Wondrous Swear Word To Color

For Stress Releasing

Charity Borsberry

Happy Coloring!

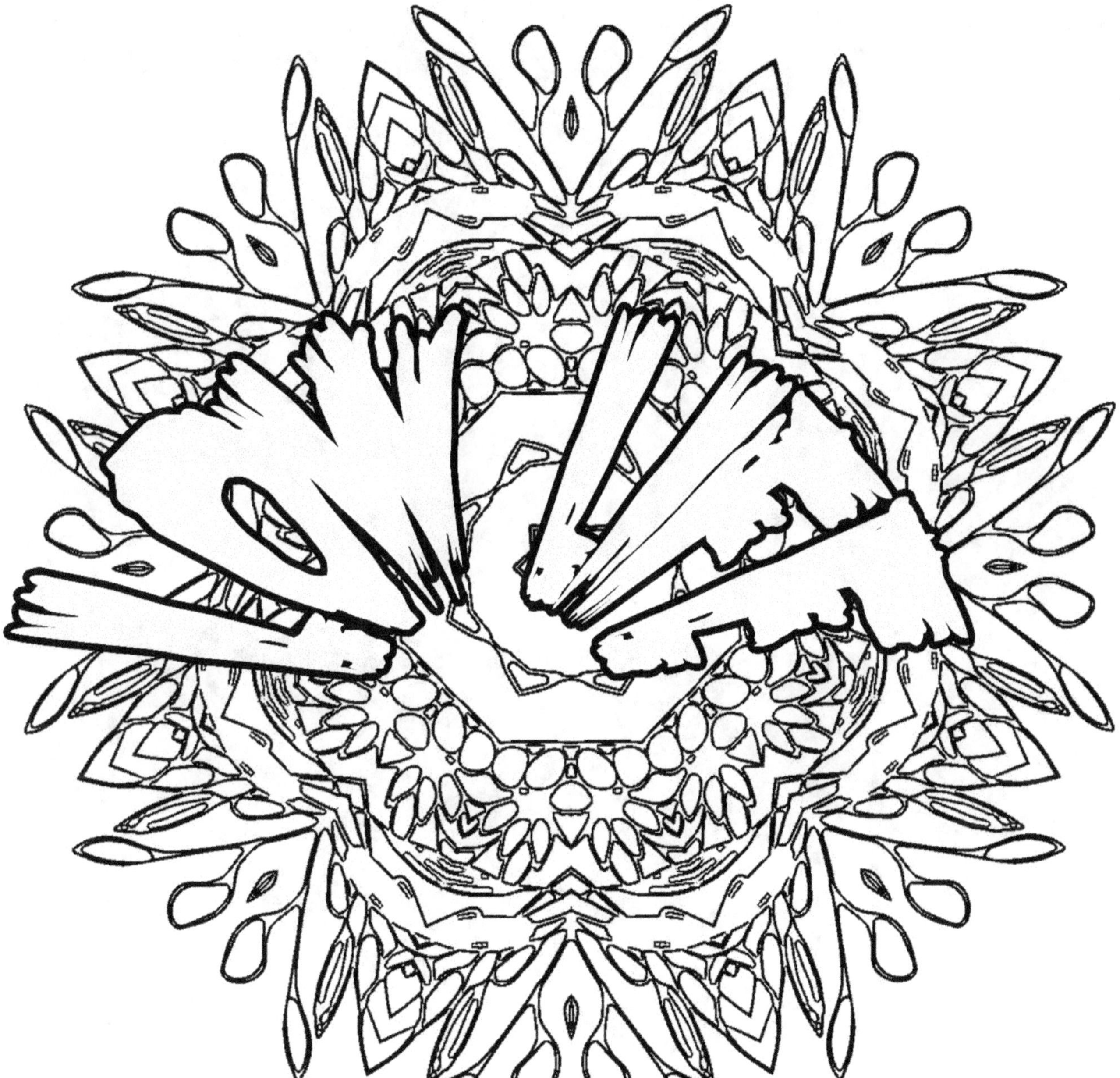

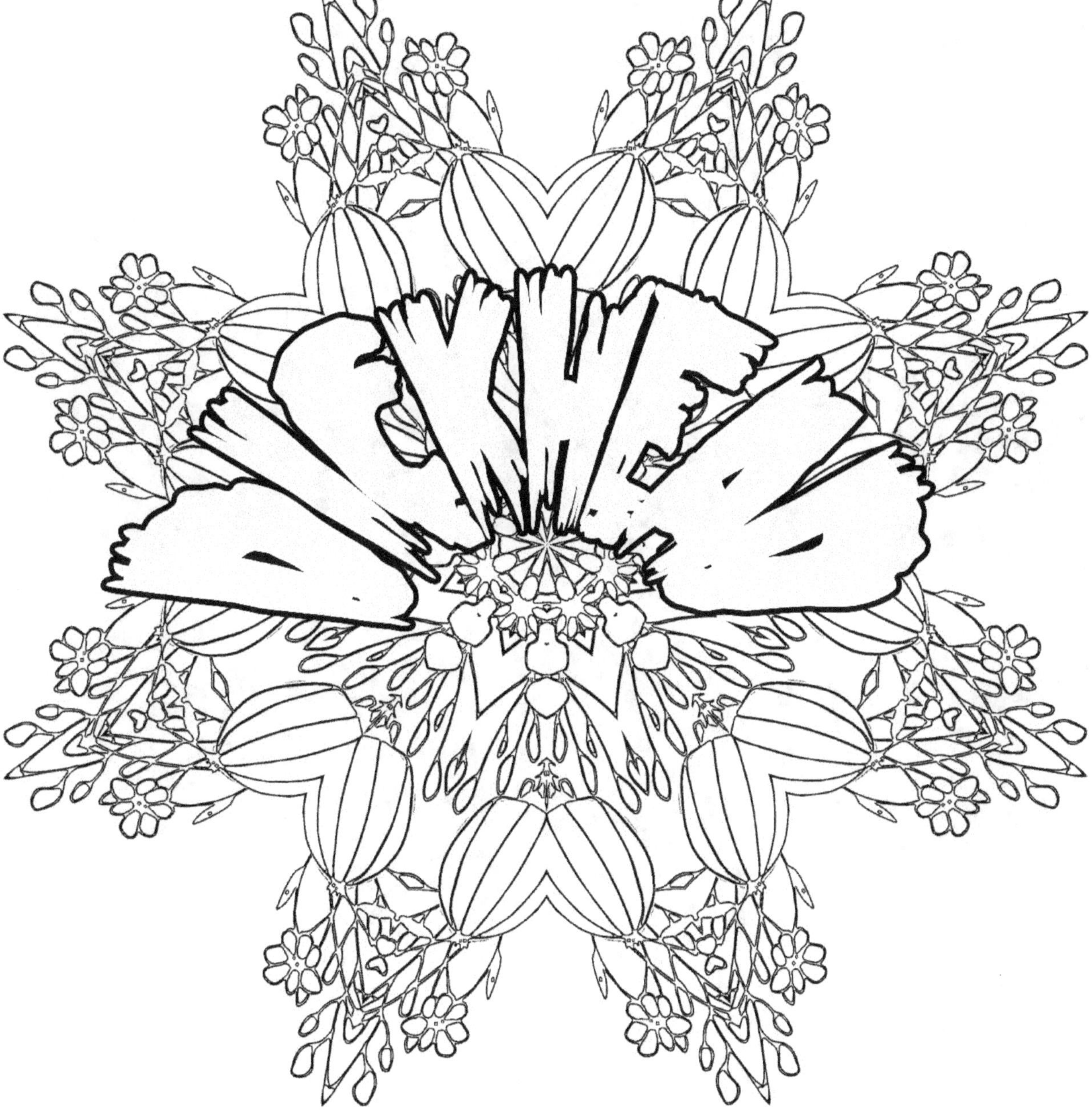

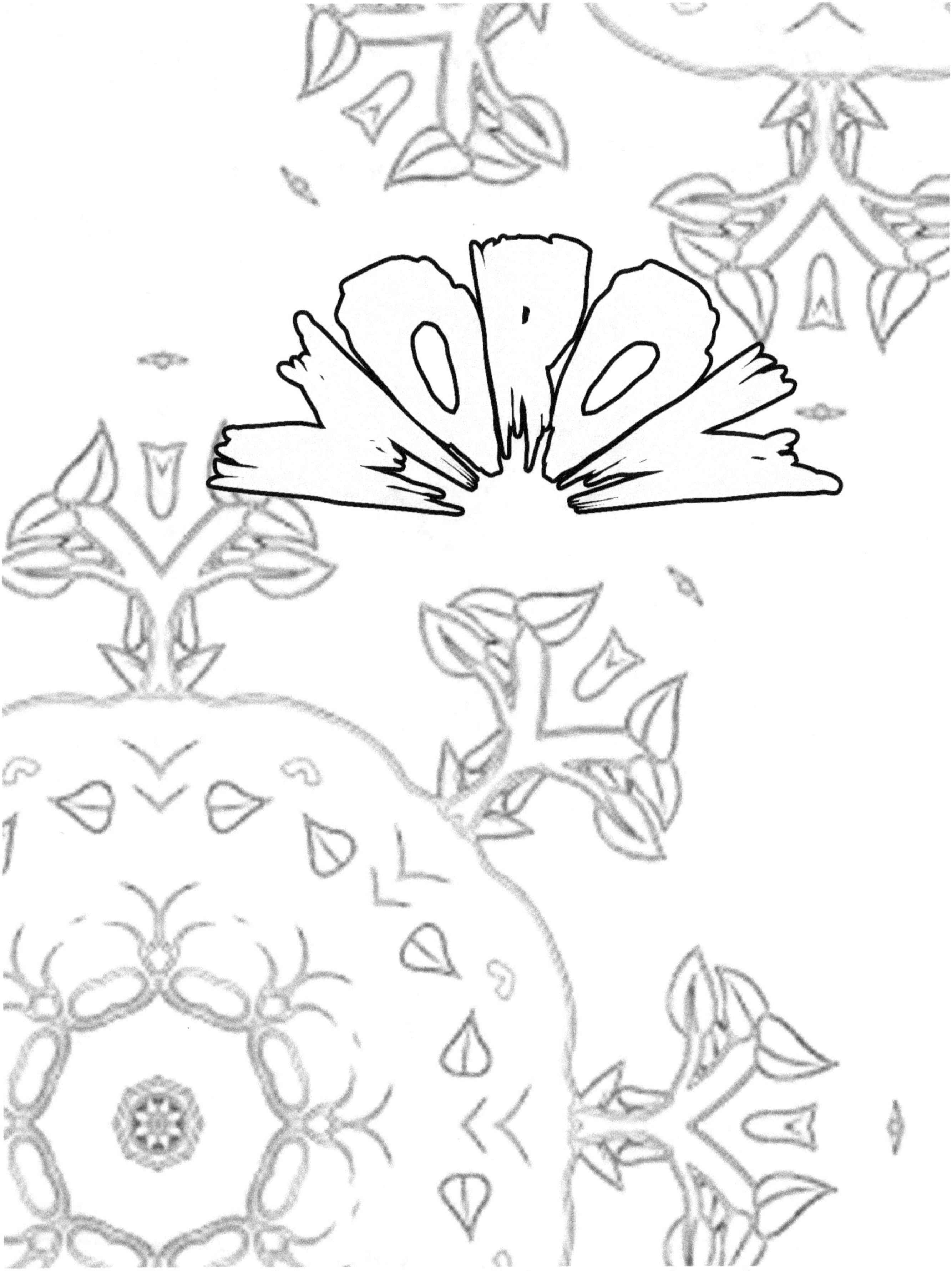

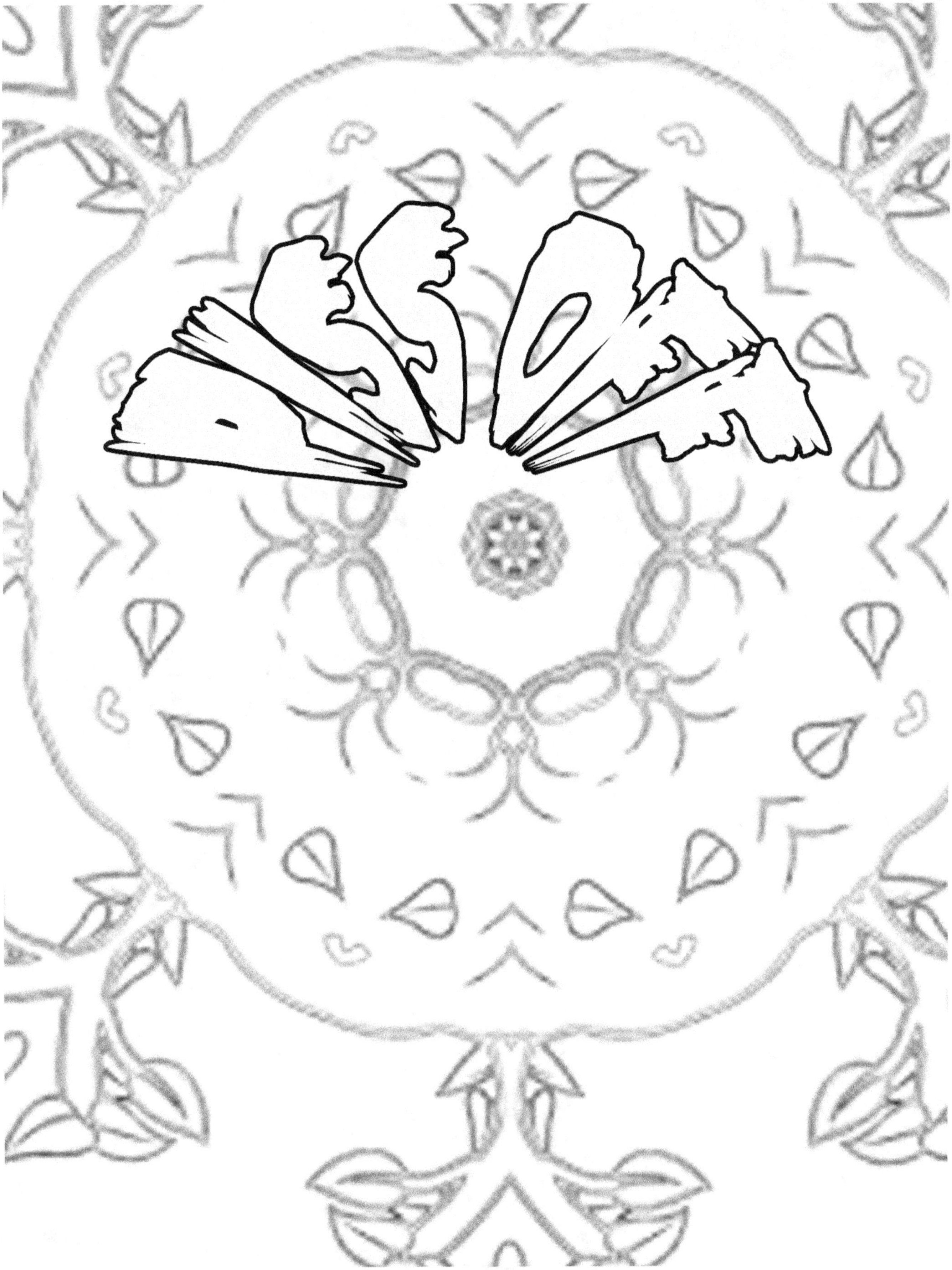

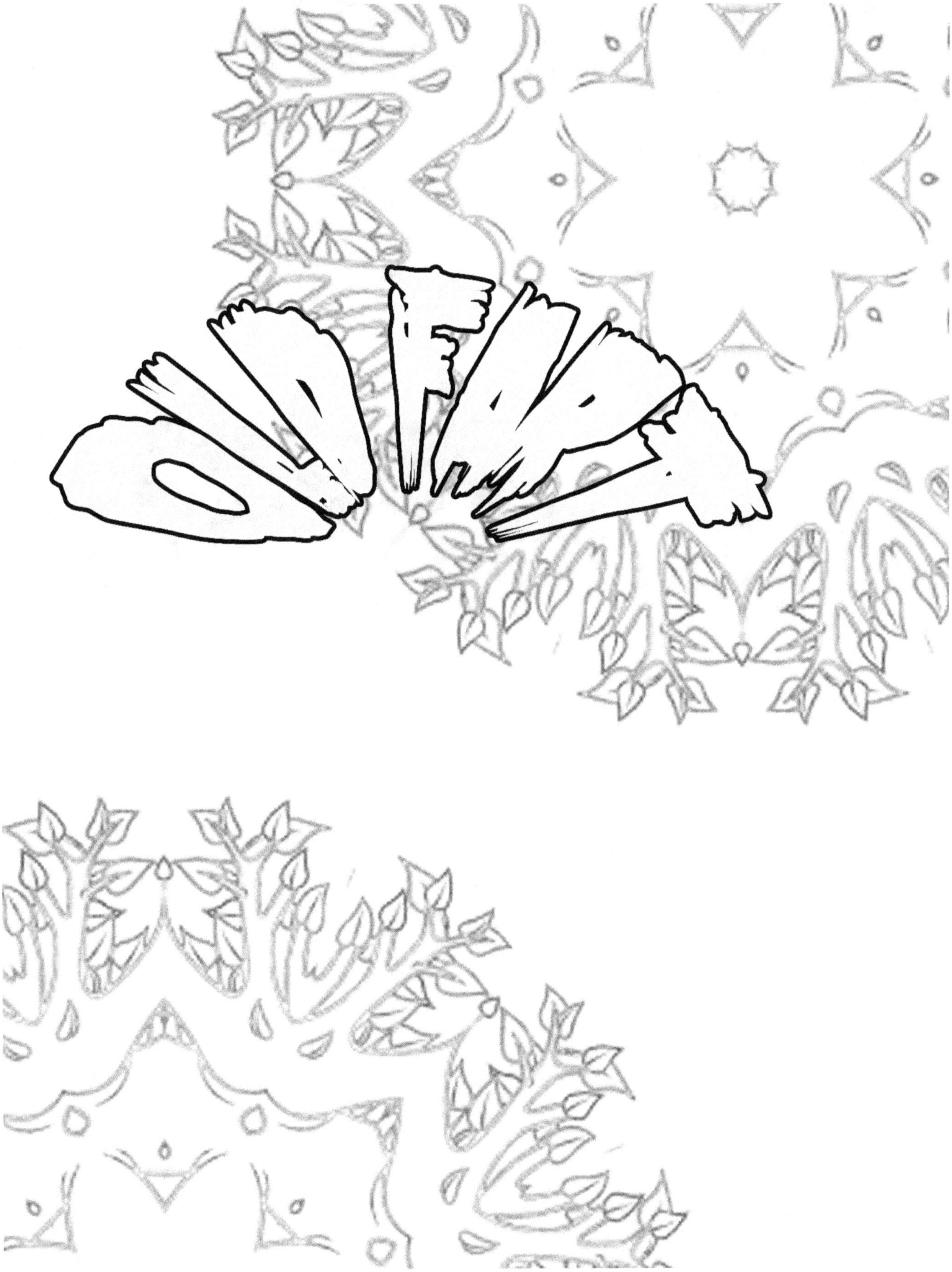

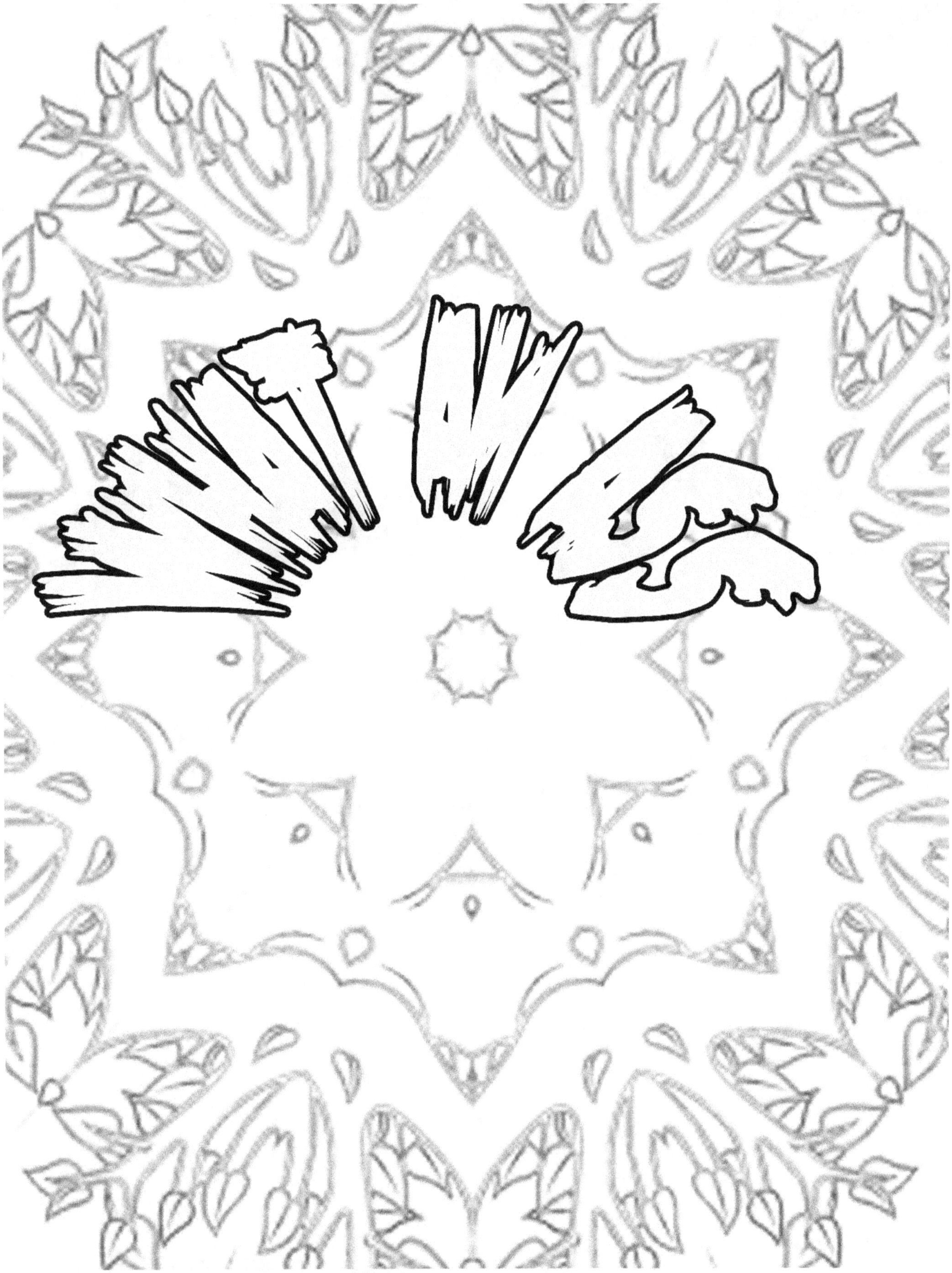

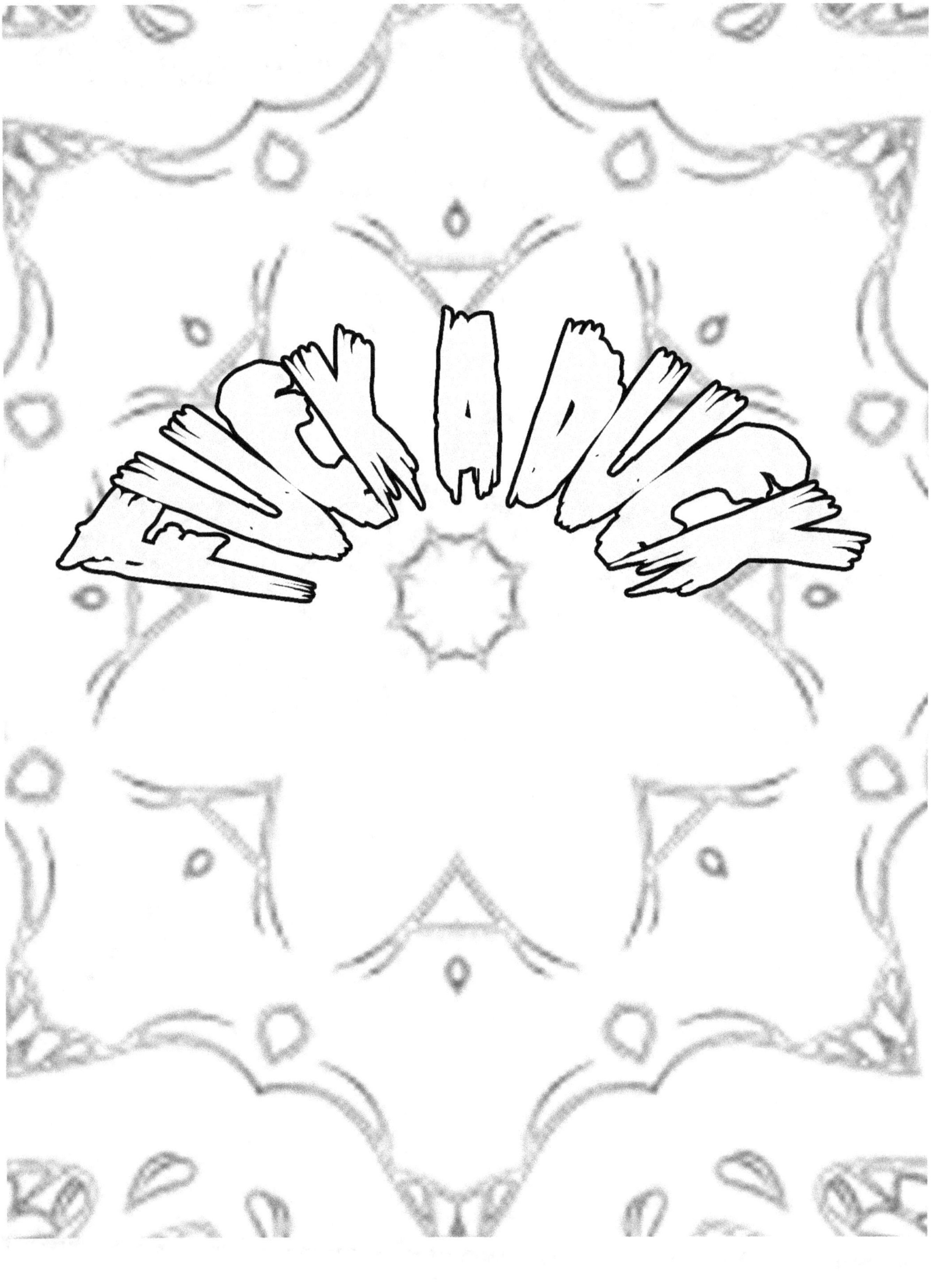
FUCK A DUCK

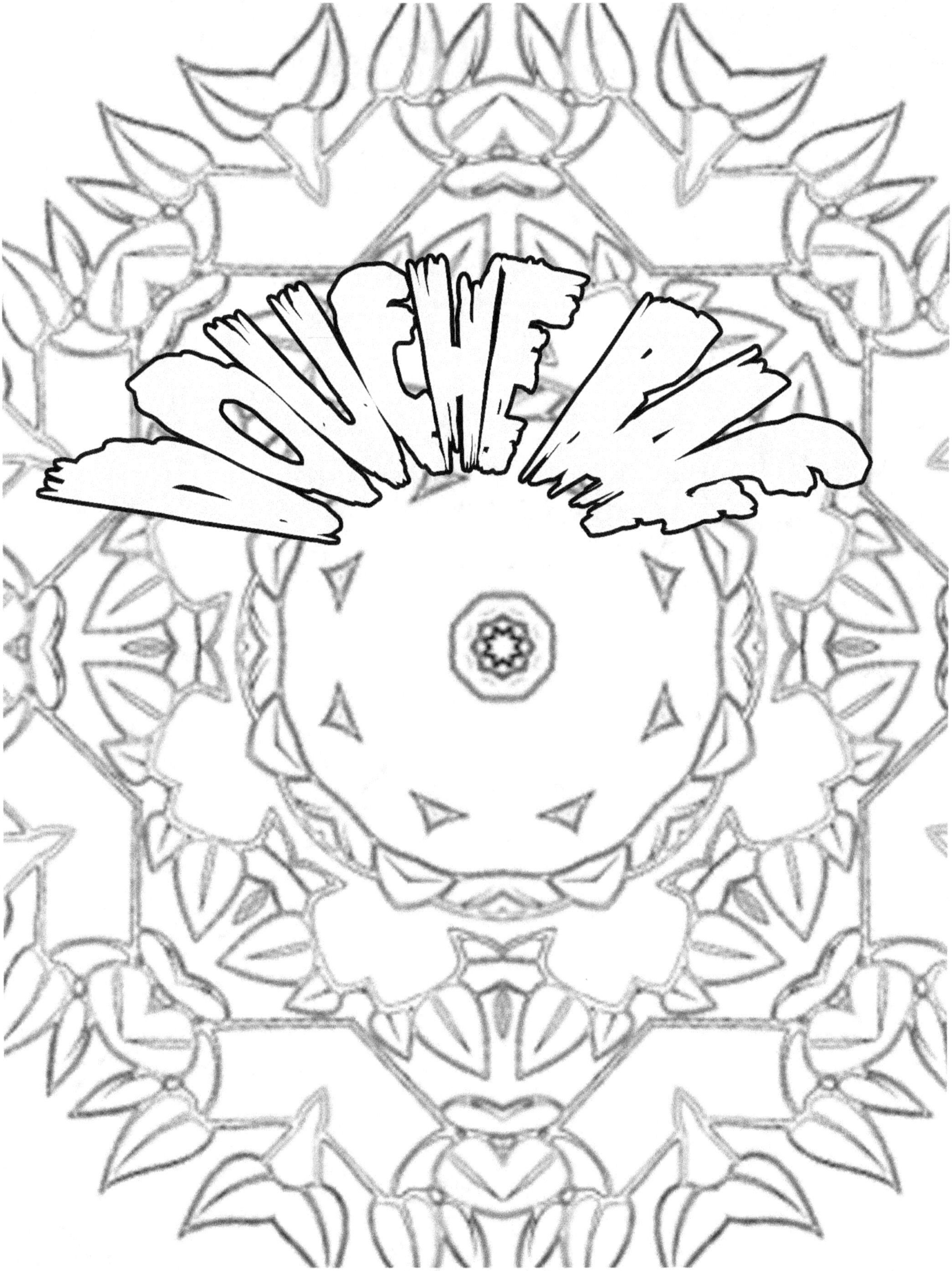
DOUCHE BAG

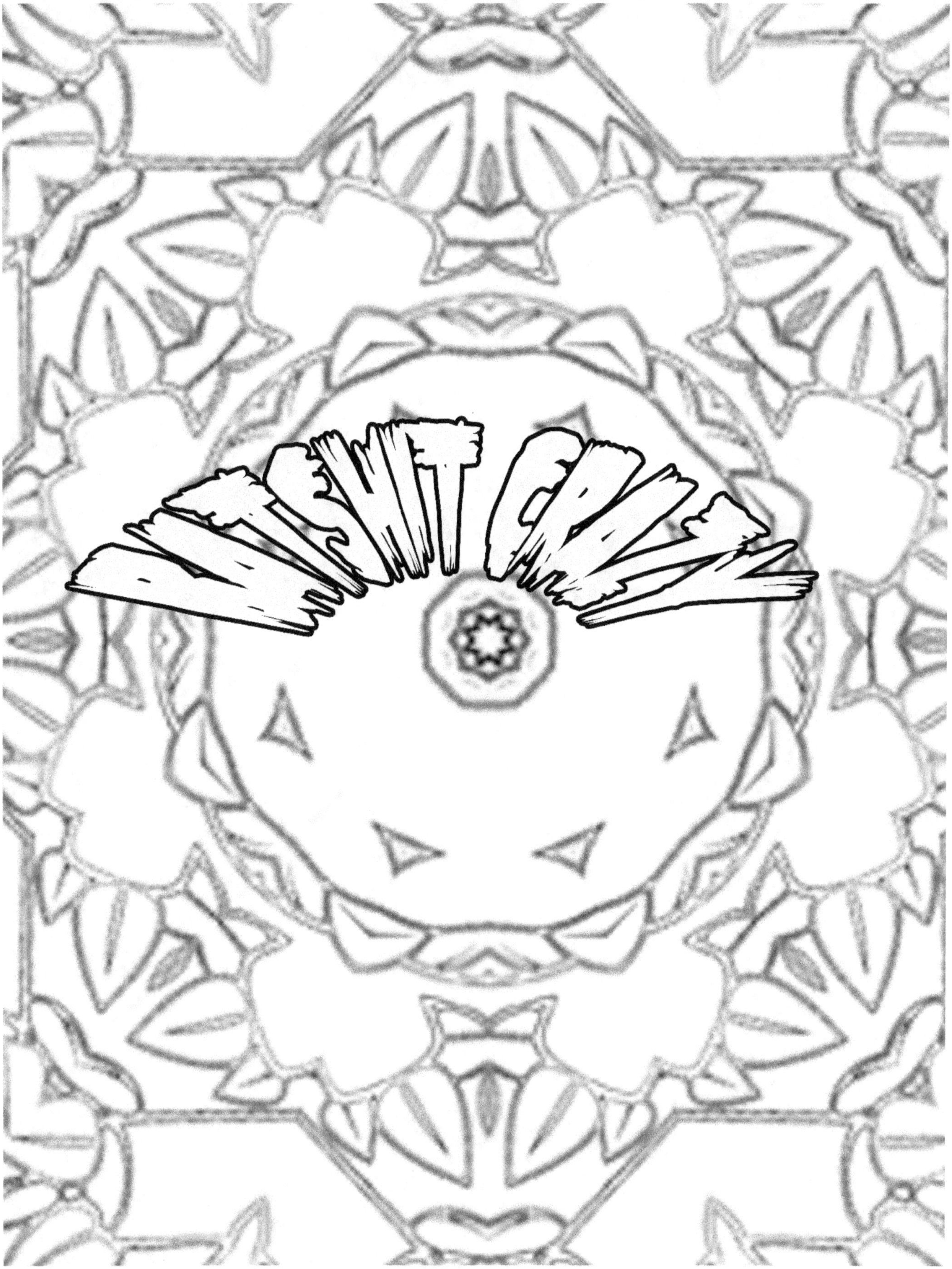
BATSHIT CRAZY

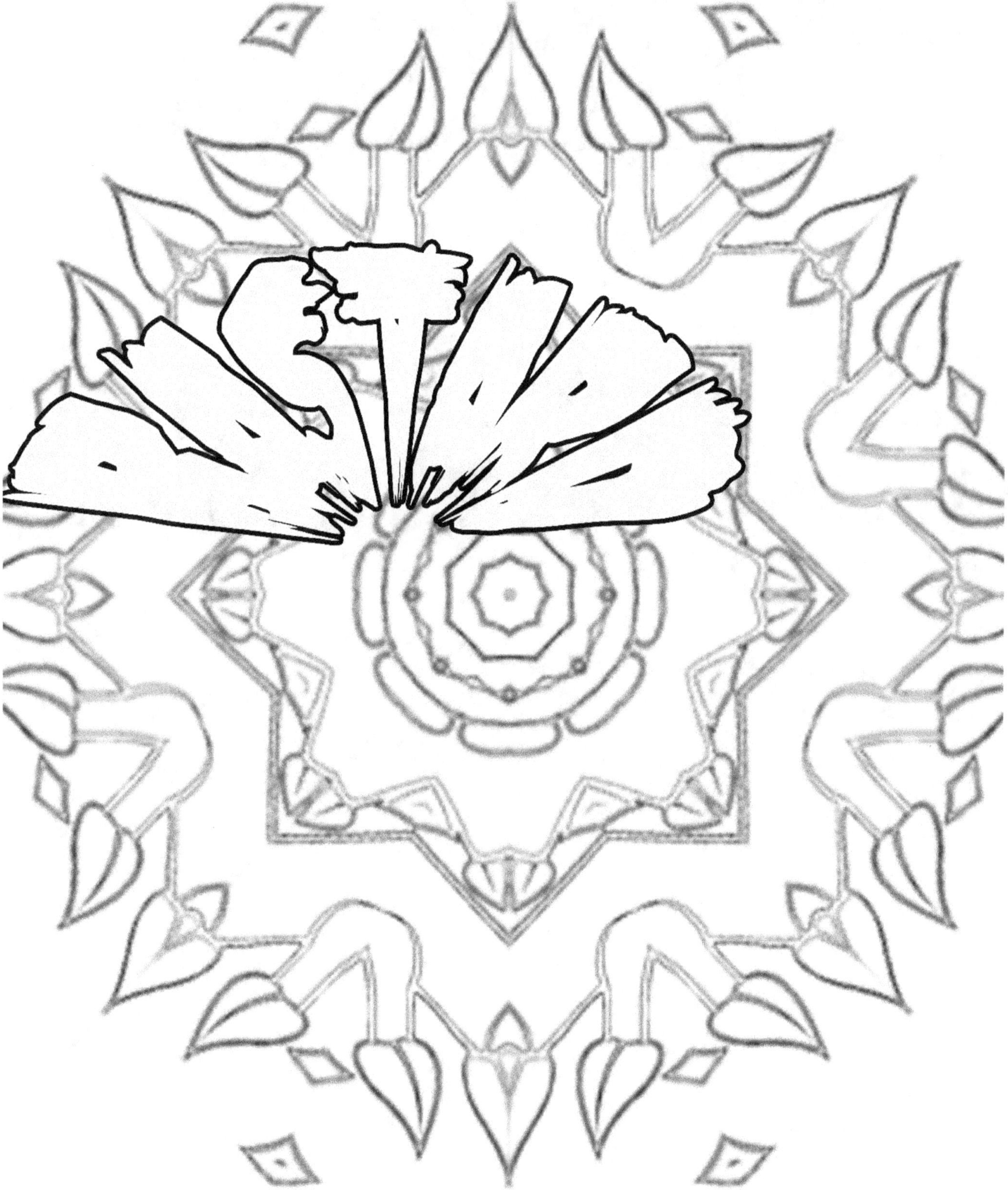

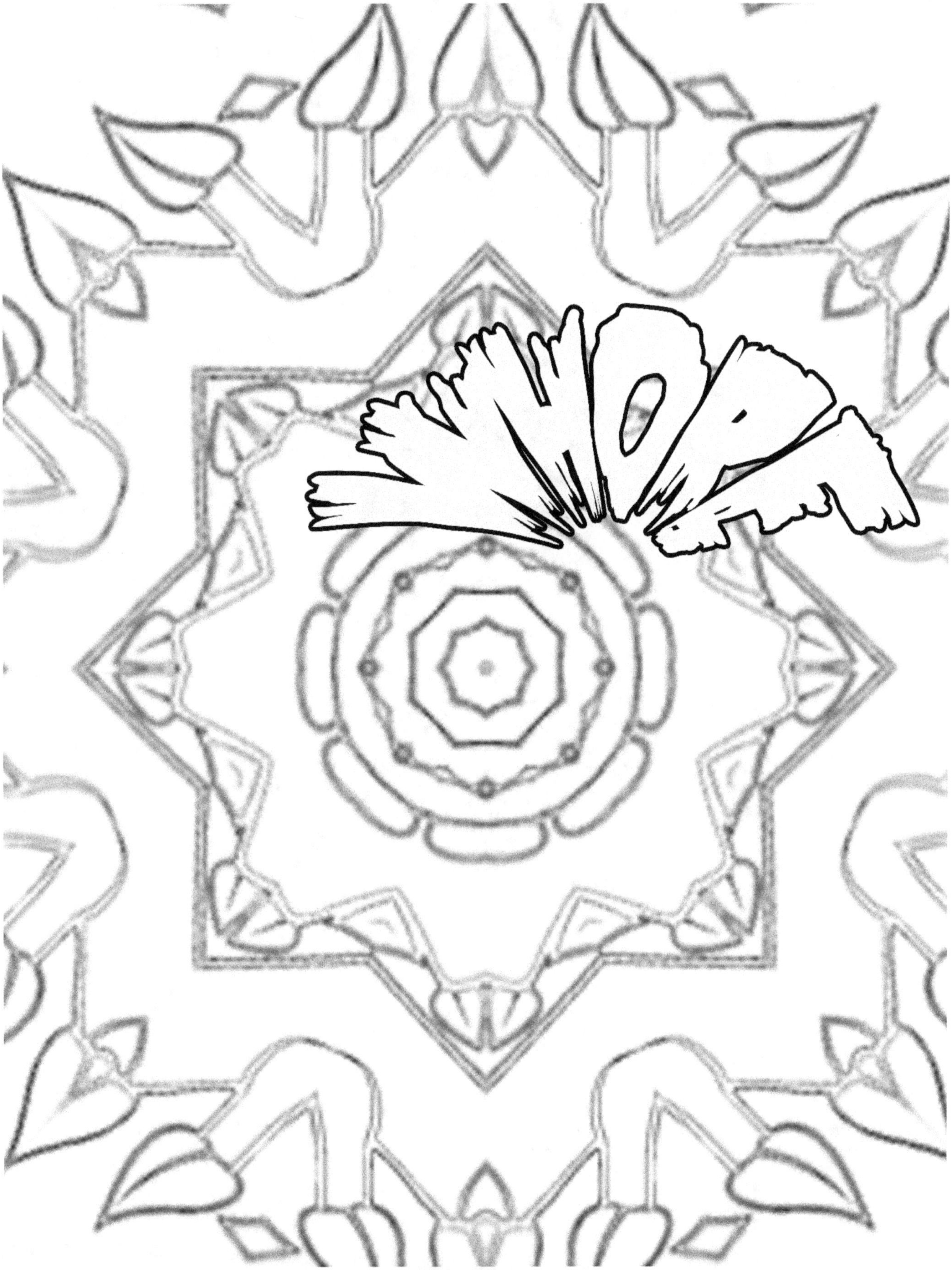

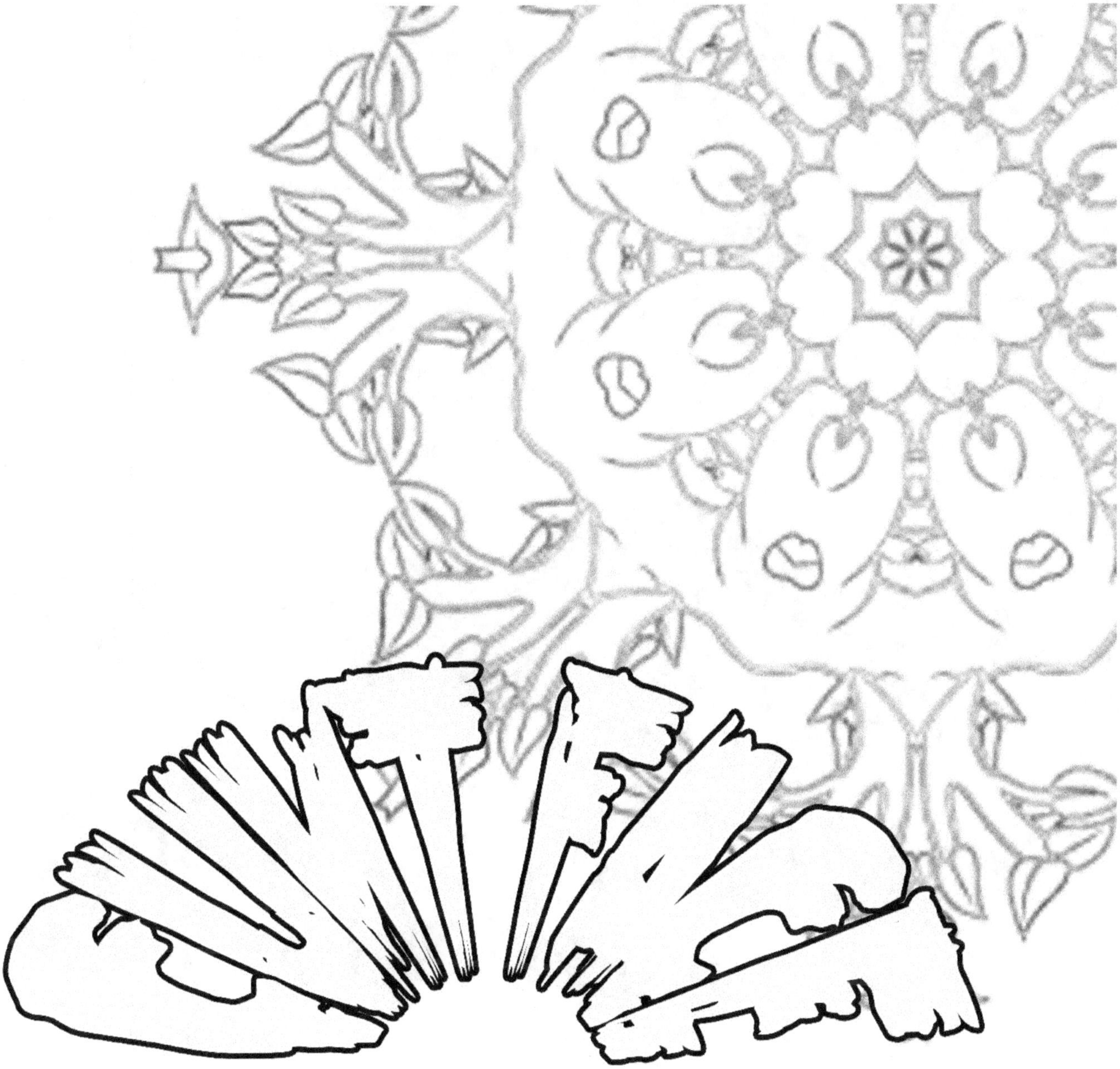

ATTENTION WHORE

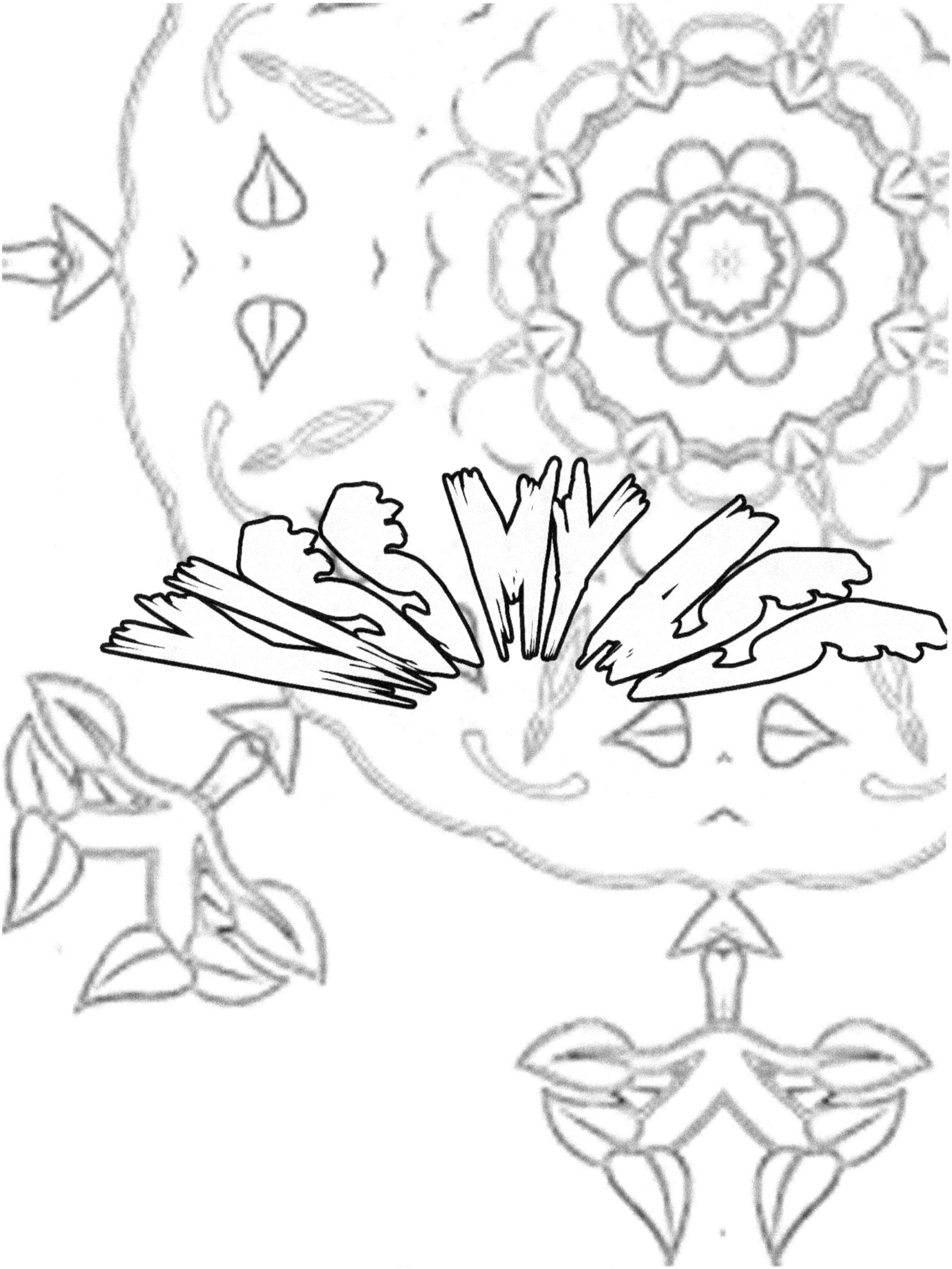

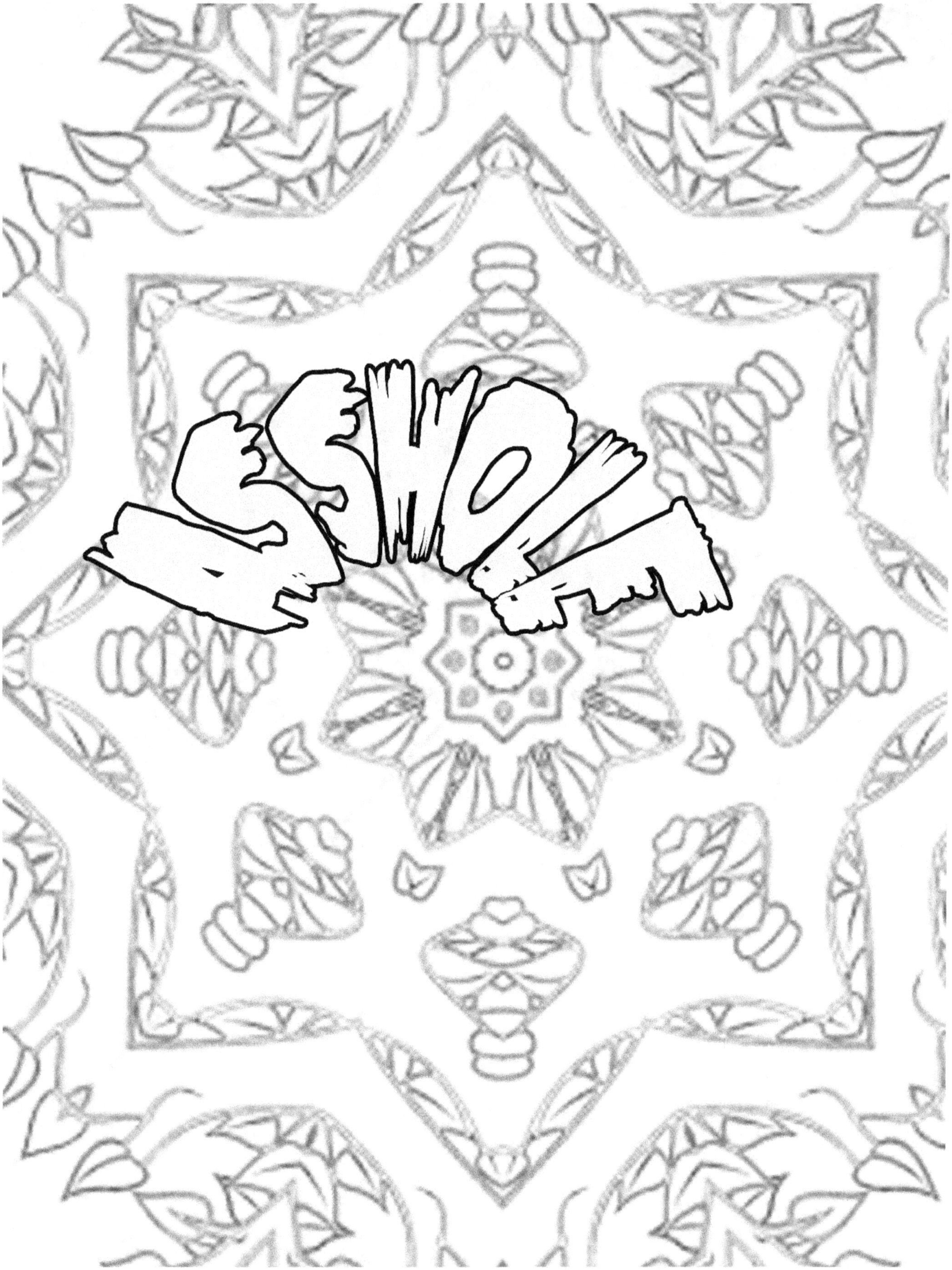
ASSHOLE

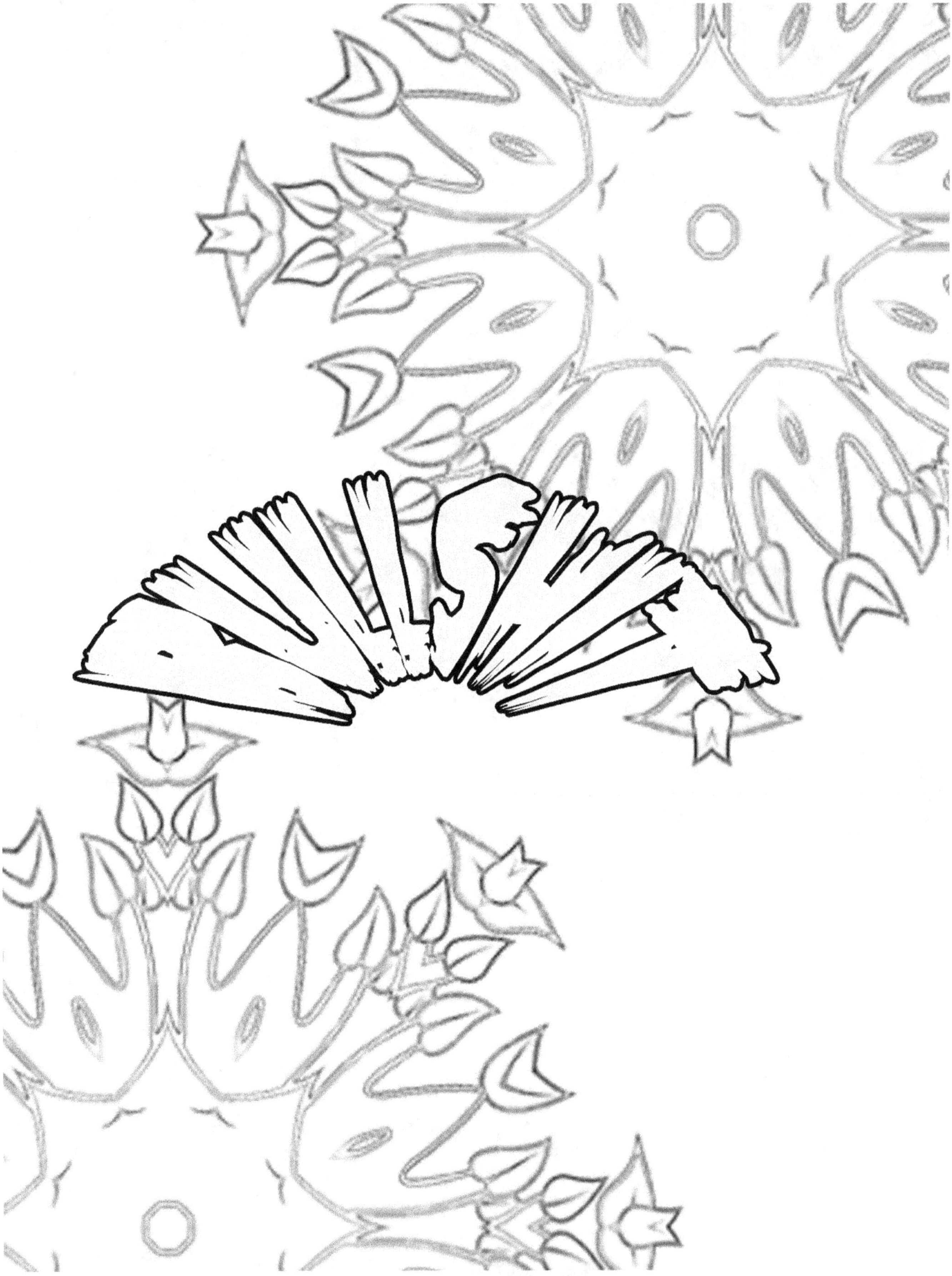

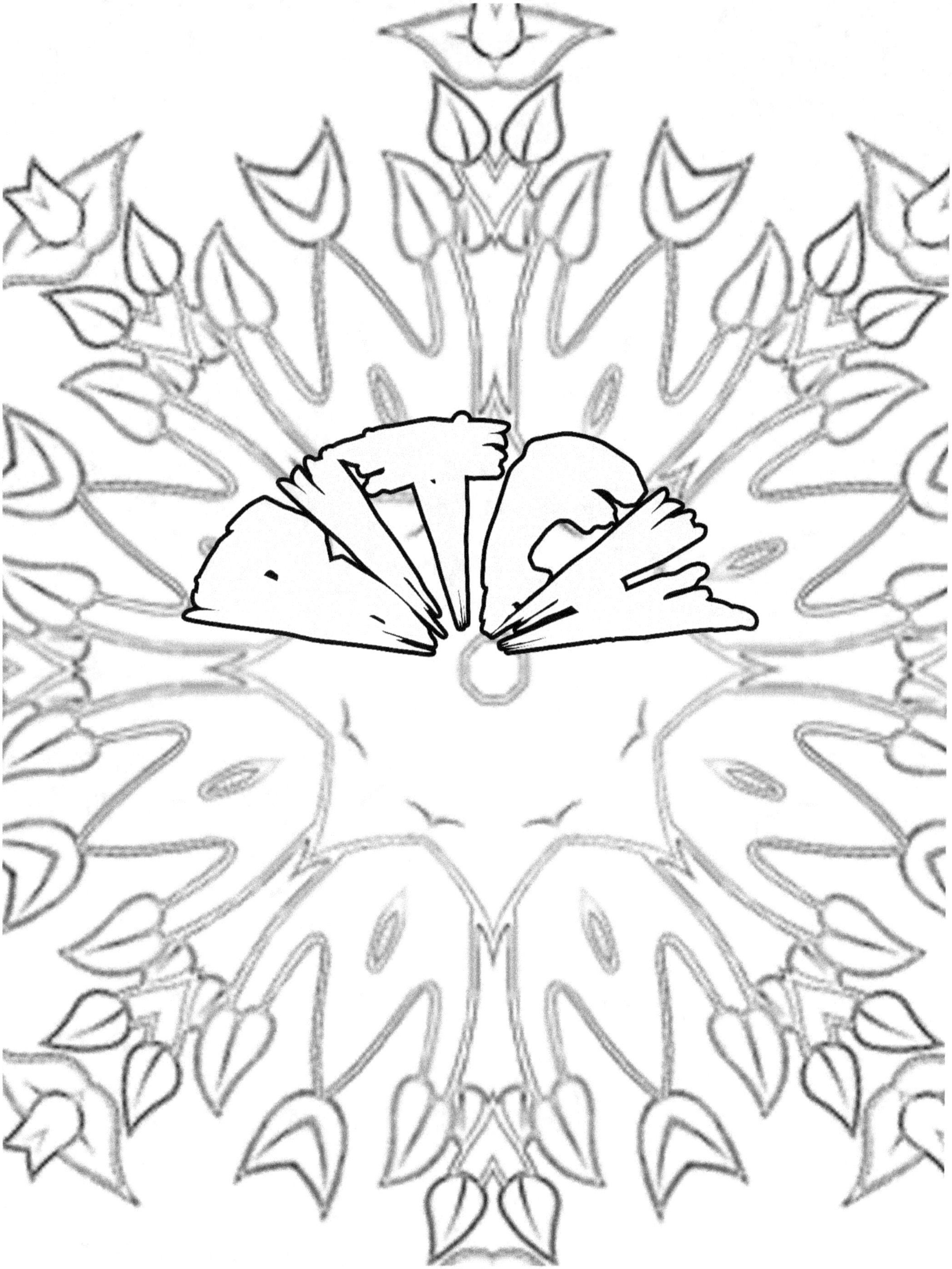

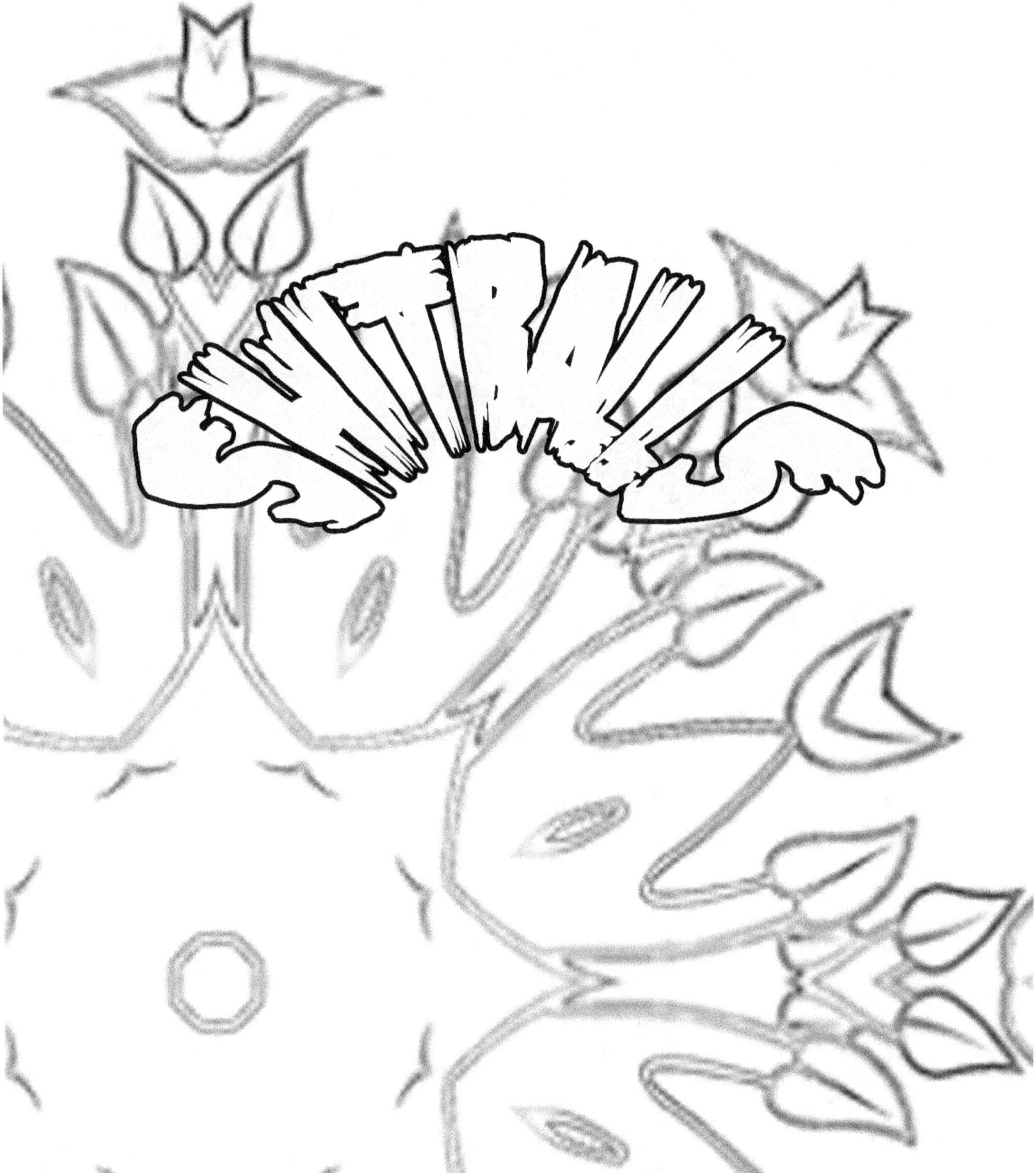

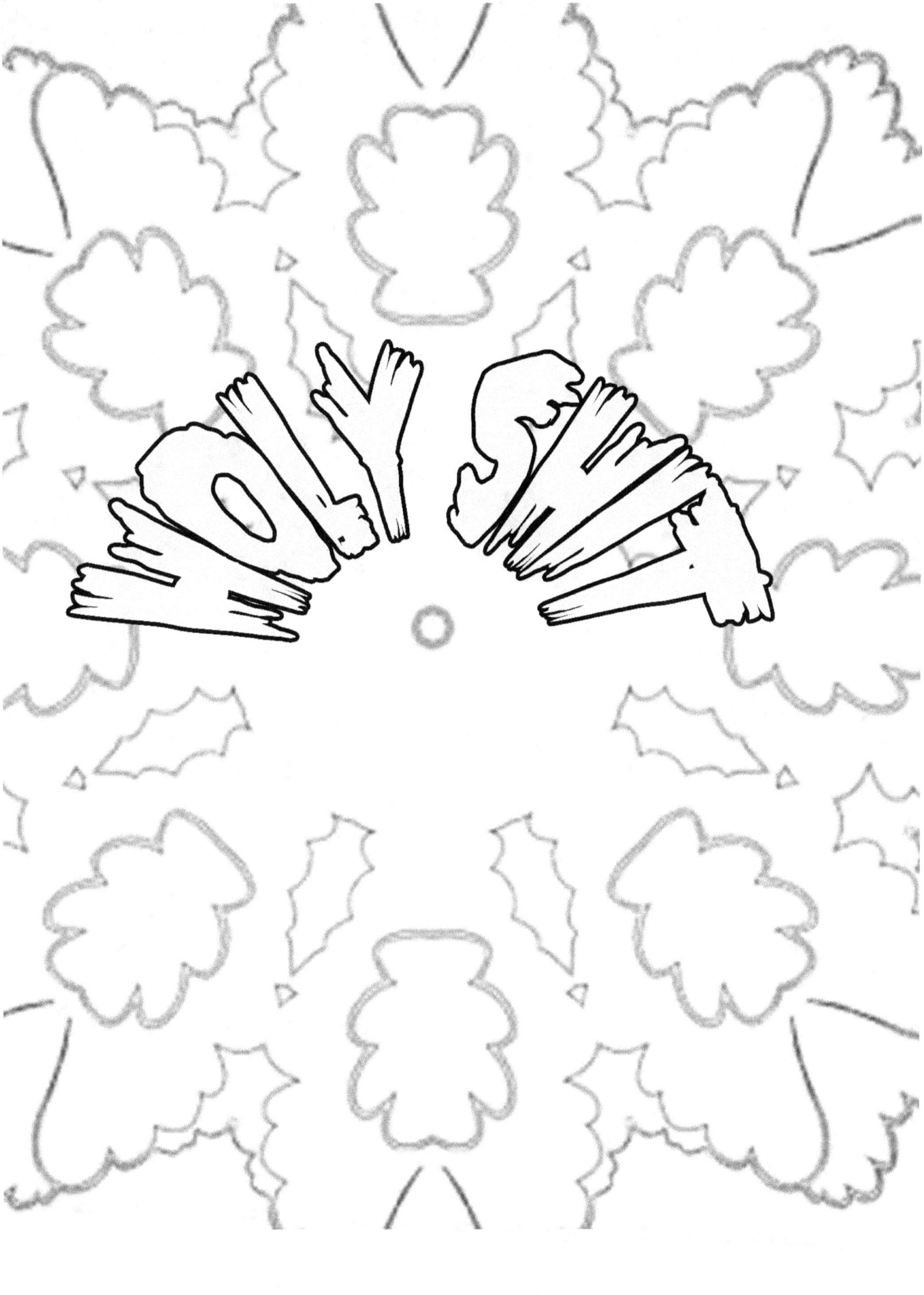
HOLY SHIT

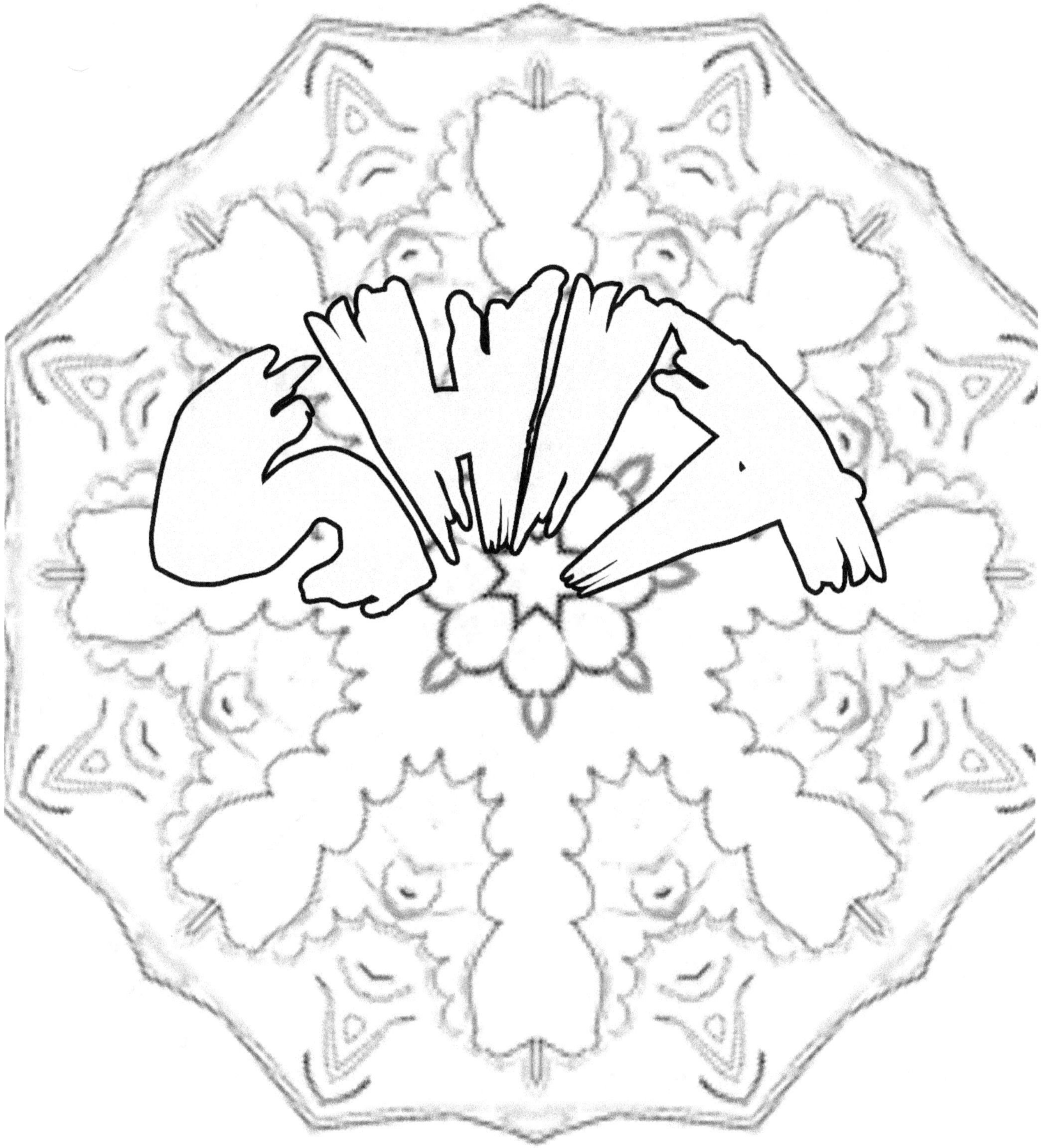
SHIT

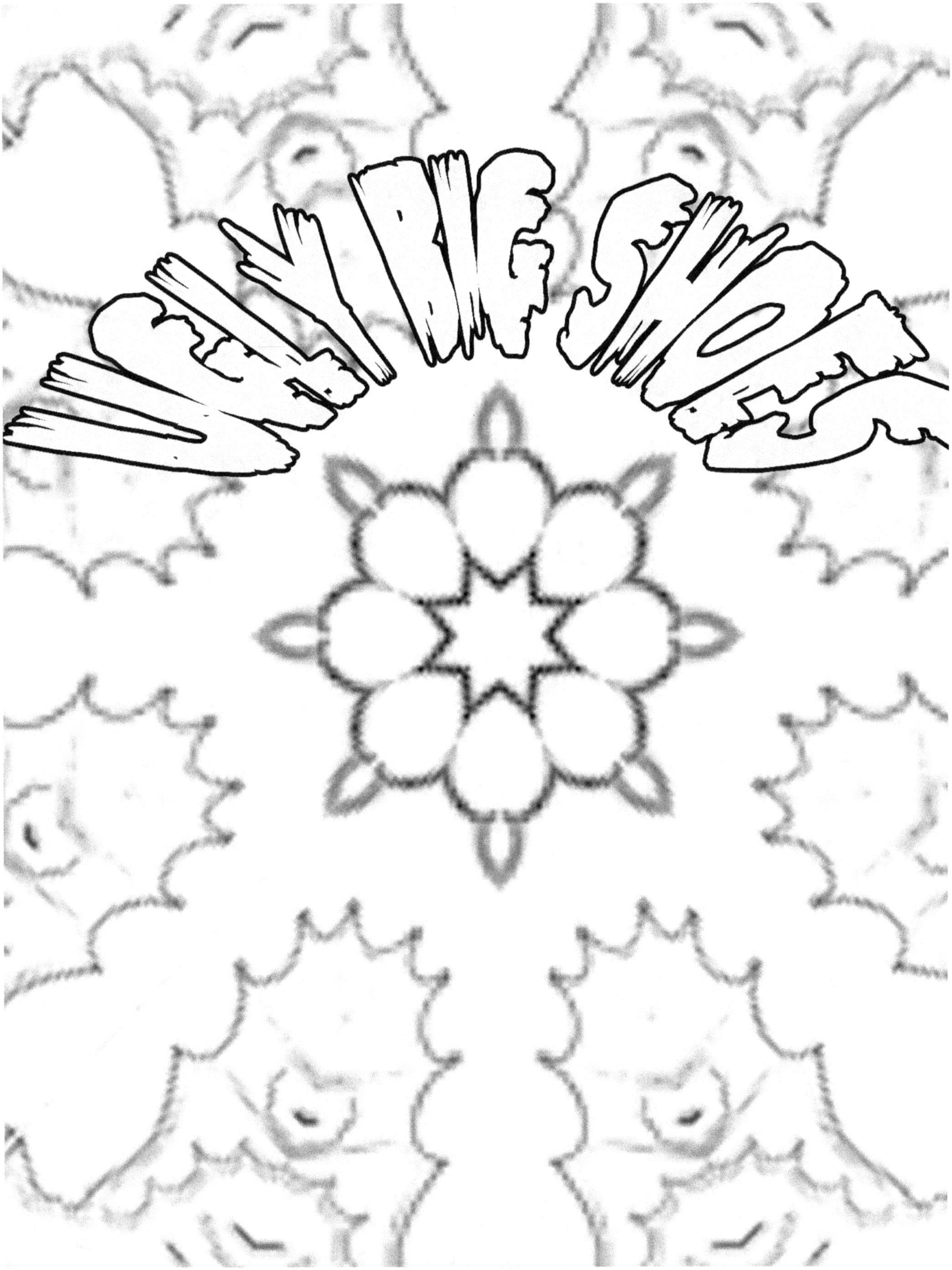
BIG SHOES

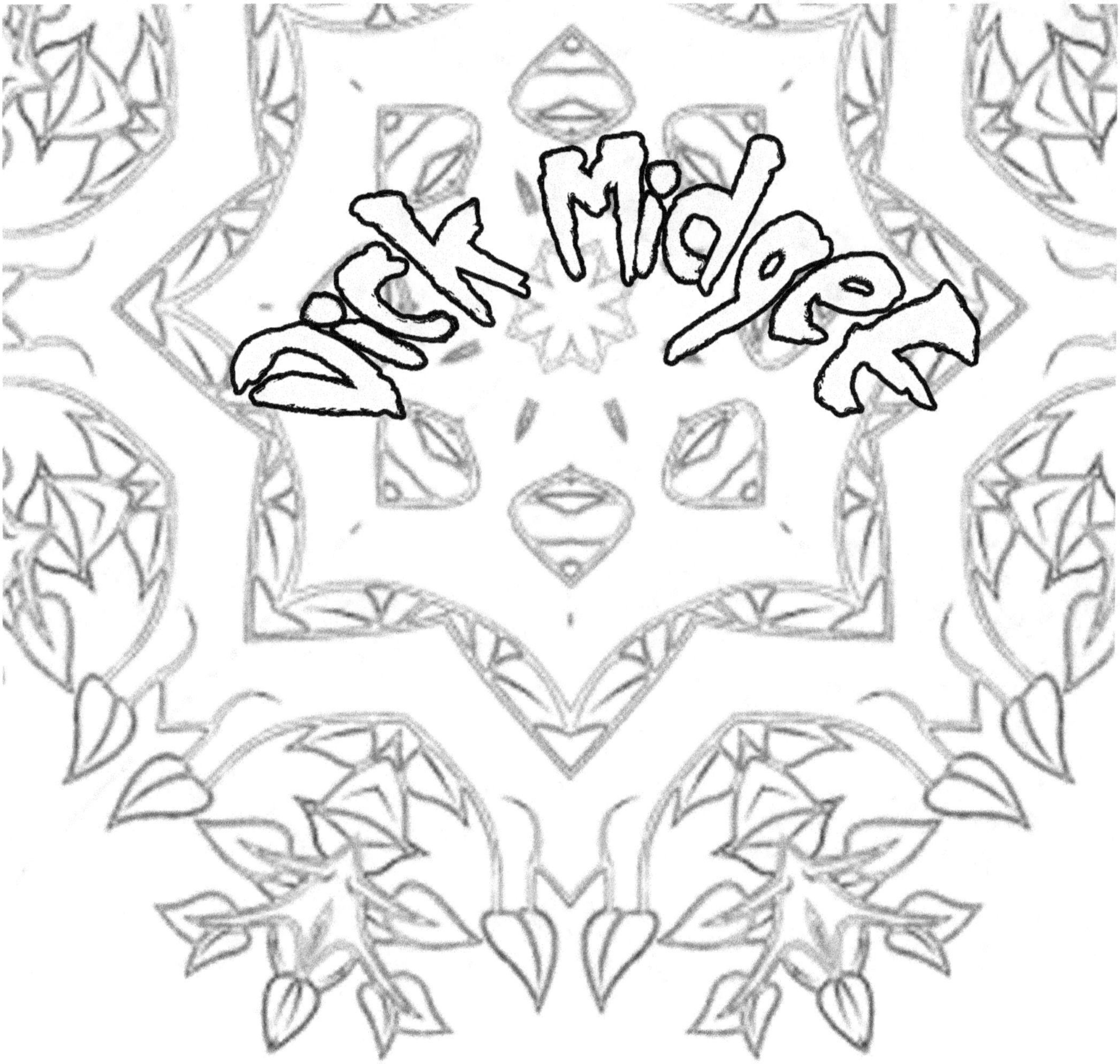
Dick Midget

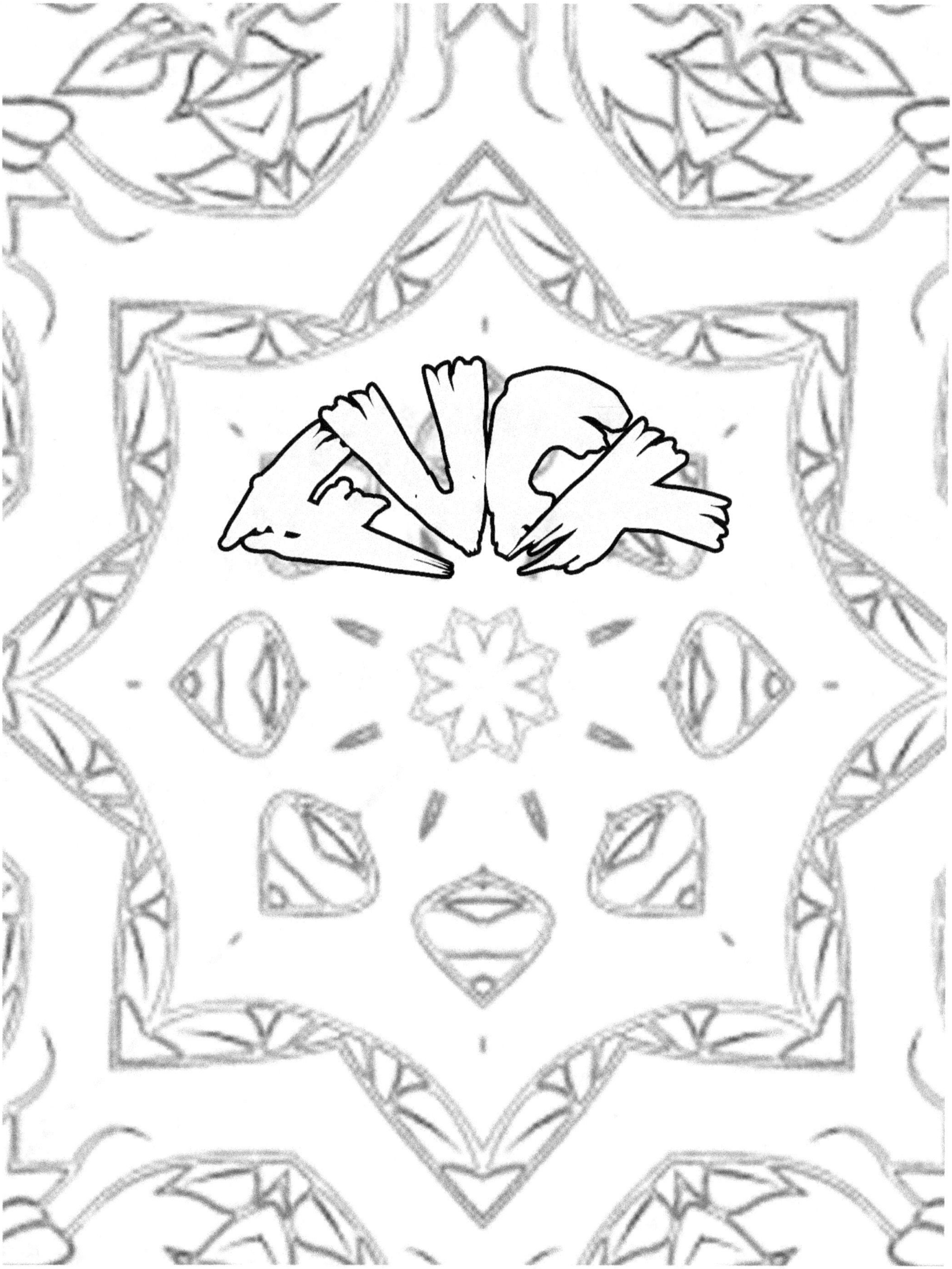

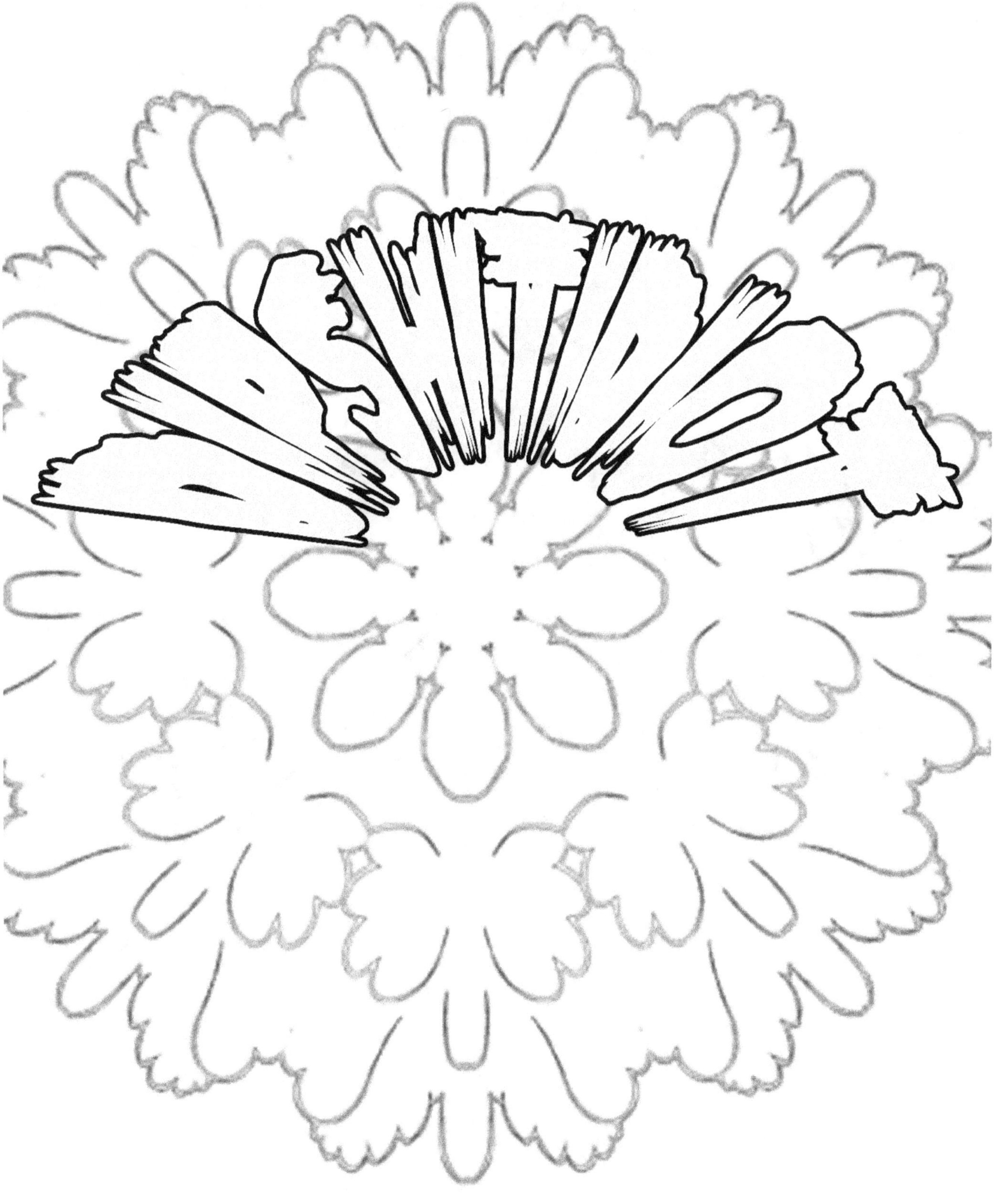

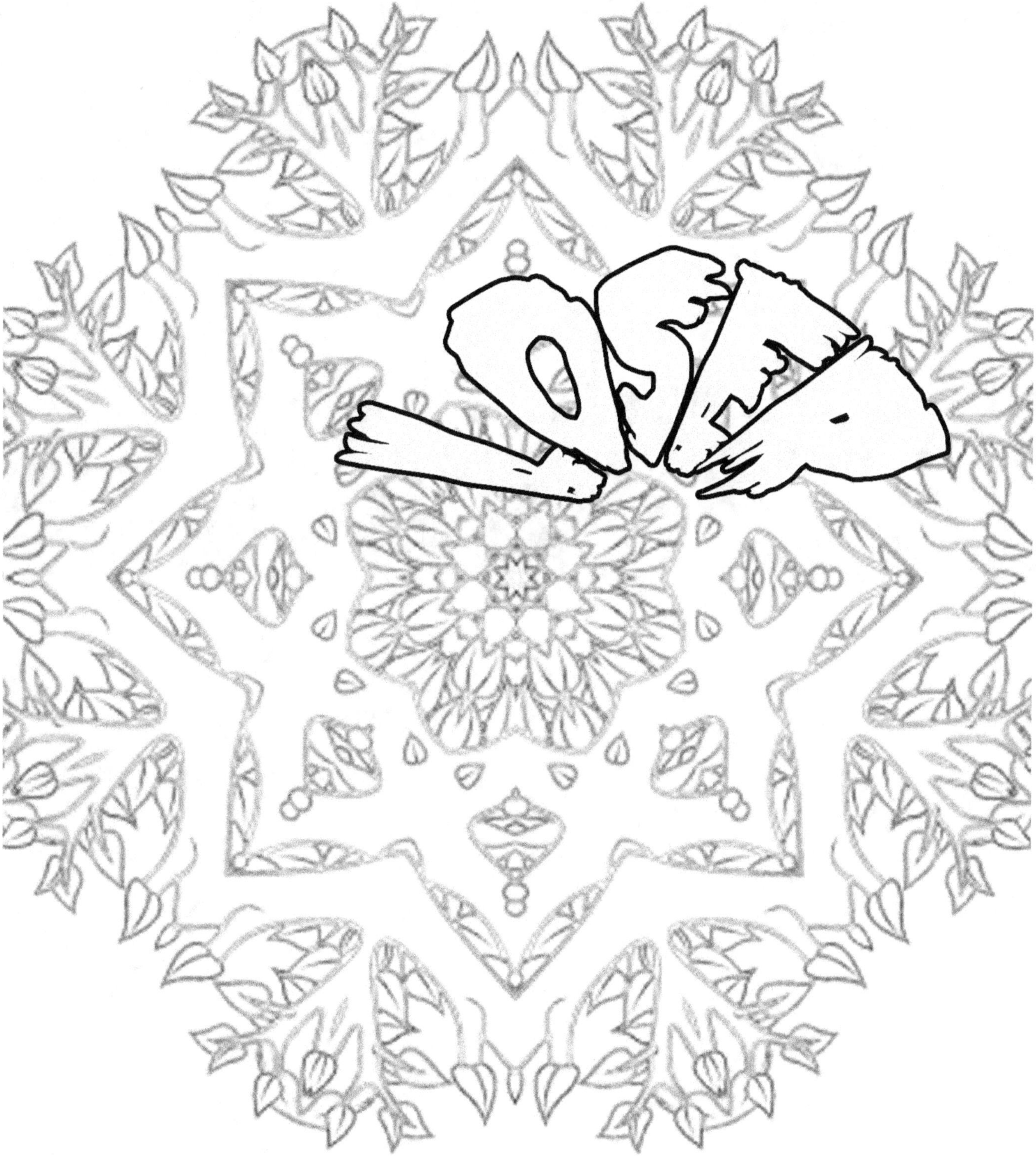

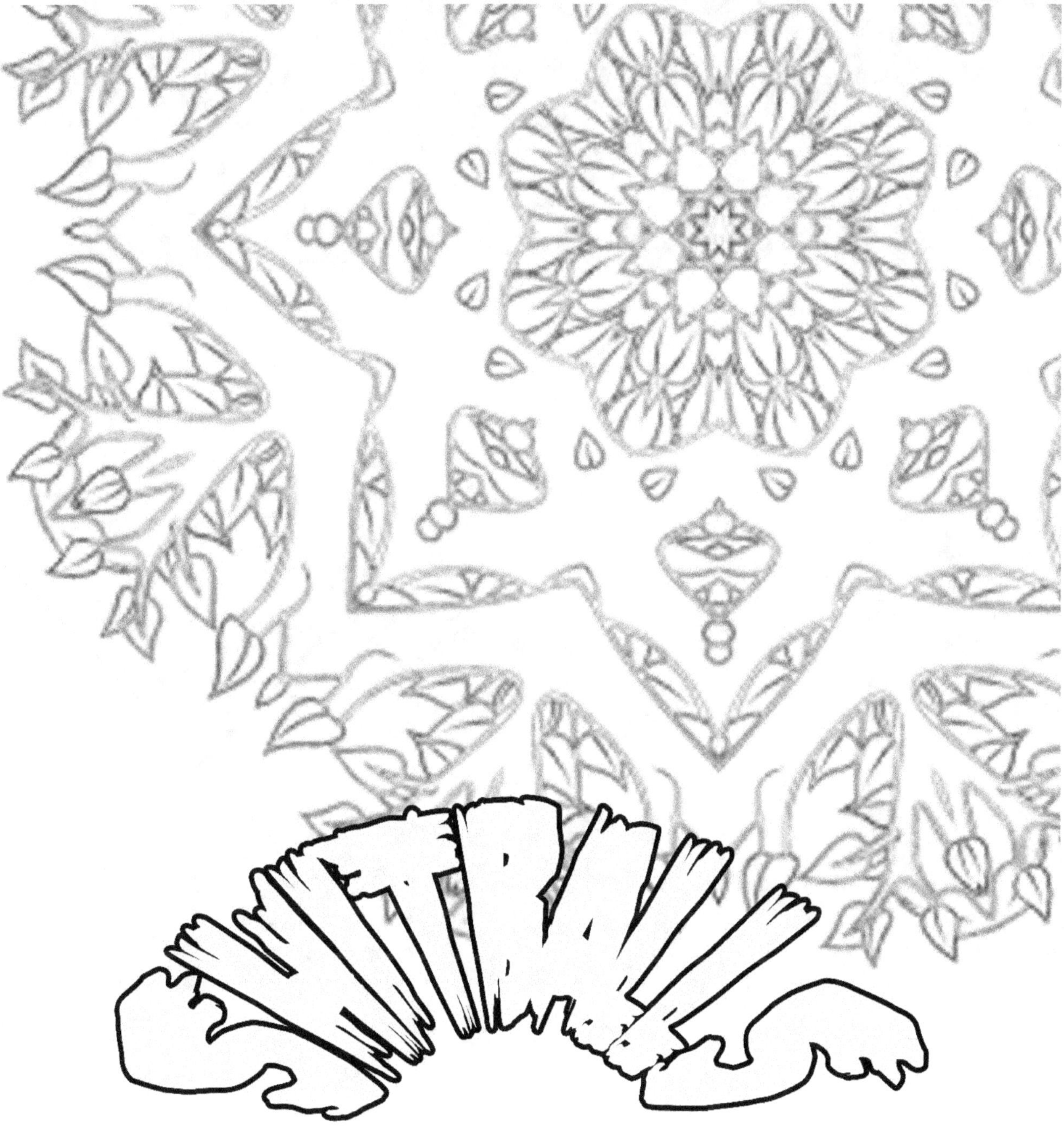

www.ingramcontent.com/pod-product-compliance
Lightning Source LLC
Chambersburg PA
CBHW081743170526
45167CB00009B/3917
9781544087191